HARRY CARAY
Voice of the Fans

Pat Hughes

with Bruce Miles

SOURCEBOOKS MEDIAFUSION™
AN IMPRINT OF SOURCEBOOKS, INC.®
NAPERVILLE, ILLINOIS

Published by Sourcebooks MediaFusion, an imprint of Sourcebooks, Inc.
P.O. Box 4410, Naperville, Illinois 60567-4410
(630) 961-3900
Fax: (630) 961-2168
www.sourcebooks.com

All efforts have been made by the editors to contact the copyright holders for the material used in this book. The editors regret if any omissions have occurred and will correct any such errors in future editions of this book.

Photos courtesy of: Pat Caray and the Caray family: pages 26, 26, 27, 30, 31, 39, 44, 50; Pat Hughes: pages 2, 3, 12, 24, 33, 77, 102, 103, 106, 107, 108, 111, 112, 118; © Steve Green: page 57; AP/WIDE WORLD PHOTOS: 6, 7, 9, 15, 22, 36, 38, 39, 40, 45, 56, 62, 64, 66, 70, 71, 84, 85, 86, 88, 100, 101, 110, 114, 117; © Bettman/Corbis: pages 10, 13, 14, 16, 18, 20, 21, 41, 46, 47, 48, 49, 51, 54, 55, 58, 60, 65, 76, 79, 80, 83 © Bracephoto.com: page 28; Chicago Tribune: pages vi, 4, 19, 27, 32, 34, 42, 52, 61, 63, 65, 68, 69, 72, 74, 78, 82, 89, 90, 91, 92, 94, 95, 96, 98, 104, 105, 116, 119

Library of Congress Cataloging-in-Publication Data

Hughes, Pat
  Harry Caray : voice of the fans / Pat Hughes.
     p. cm.
  1. Caray, Harry. 2. Sportscasters–United States–Biography. I. Title.

GV742.42.C37H84 2007
070.4'49796092–dc22
[B]
                                   2007022869

Printed and bound in the United States of America.
RRD 10 9 8 7 6 5 4 3 2

FROM PAT HUGHES:

To my mother, Mary Margaret Hughes, who along with my father, the late Vergil Herbert Hughes, always stressed to me the importance of reading and learning

FROM BRUCE MILES:

For my family

ACKNOWLEDGMENTS

Pat would like to thank the following people for helping to make this production possible: Bud Selig, the Commissioner of Major League Baseball; Dutchie Caray and the entire family of Harry Caray, with a special acknowledgment to Skip Caray and Chip Caray; the Chicago Cubs organization, with a sincere thank you to John McDonough, president; WGN Radio and WGN Television; Ron Santo and Thom Brennaman; the St. Louis Cardinals organization; KMOX Radio; a sincere thank you to Curt Smith, America's foremost baseball broadcasting authority and author of both *Voices of the Game* and *Voices of Summer*; Bob Verdi, along with Harry Caray, author of the book *Holy Cow!*; Steve Stone with Barry Rozner, authors of the book *Where's Harry?*; the National Baseball Hall of Fame, with special thanks to Jeff Idelson, Jeremy Jones, and Scot Mondore. Some of the recordings on the CD are courtesy of the National Baseball Hall of Fame library and are available to the public. Additional audio cuts provided by: John Miley, sports broadcast historian and president of the Miley collection; George Castle, sports journalist and author; Ted Patterson, sportscasting historian. And thanks to Gary Pressy, Wrigley Field organist, for his rendition of "Take Me Out to the Ball Game." And thank you to Steven Leventhal, engineer at the studios of SRN Broadcasting, Lake Bluff, Illinois. A special thank you to Bruce Miles for his literary talent, agreeable attitude, and friendship. And the biggest thanks of all to my family: my wife Trish, and my daughters Janell and Amber.

Bruce would like to thank Pat Hughes for the opportunity to work with him on such a fun project. Someday soon, Pat will be a Hall of Famer. The Chicago Cubs and their media relations department get a nod for the historical information they provided. And no project gets done without the support—and the occasional push—from one's family.

CONTENTS

Preface 1

1 Voice of the Fans, *CD Track 1* 5

2 The 1984 Cubs, *CD Track 2* 11

3 The 1964 Cardinals, *CD Track 3* 17

4 Harry's Childhood, *CD Track 4* 25

5 Joliet and Kalamazoo, *CD Track 5* 29

6 Cardinals Radio, *CD Track 6* 35

7 Show Business and Fun, *CD Track 7* 43

8 Oakland, *CD Track 8* 53

9 White Sox, *CD Track 9* 59

10 "Take Me Out to the Ball Game," *CD Track 10* 67

11 The Cubs, *CD Track 11* 75

12 The President Is On Line One, *CD Track 12* 81

13 The 1989 Cubs, *CD Track 13* 87

14 Cooperstown, *CD Track 14* 93

15 Personal Memories, *CD Track 15* 99

16 Farewell, *CD Track 16* 115

PREFACE

THE BASEBALL HALL OF FAME broadcasters are a group of men I greatly admire.

Growing up in San Jose, California, I was raised on the voices of the San Francisco Giants, Russ Hodges and Lon Simmons. At night, I could tune in to the incomparable Vin Scully of the Los Angeles Dodgers.

Since my parents both had Missouri roots, we would take family vacations to their childhood homes. That gave me the opportunity to listen to the great Cardinals' announcers, Harry Caray and Jack Buck.

I am certain that Hall of Famers such as Vinny, Harry, Jack, Russ, and Lon inspired my interest in baseball announcing.

As I write these words in April 2007, I am on the Chicago Cubs' charter airplane bound for Atlanta, where I will broadcast the series between the Cubs and the Braves. I am in my twelfth year with the Cubs on WGN Radio and in my twenty-fifth season as a big-league baseball announcer.

A few years back, I came up with the idea of producing some tribute CDs to the great baseball announcers who have inspired, educated, and entertained me my entire life. I call the project "Baseball Voices: The Hall of Fame Series."

The first two efforts, released simultaneously, are "The Voice of the Cardinals" (Jack Buck) and "The Voice of the Fans" (Harry Caray).

These CDs include many of my favorite things: baseball, broadcasting, history, highlights, humor, storytelling, jargon, and music. While each production requires an enormous amount of work, they also are truly a labor of love. I produce each one hoping the listener will enjoy the recordings over and over. I am greatly pleased when a customer tells me that a CD "brings back great memories."

Harry Caray was a major-league baseball announcer for 53 seasons, so there are many, many memories to evoke. He was the St. Louis Cardinals'

lead announcer for 25 years. Then, after one year with the Oakland A's (1970), he moved to Chicago and broadcast for the White Sox until 1981. He then became the WGN TV and Radio voice of the Chicago Cubs from 1982 until his death in 1998. I was fortunate to work with him in his final two years.

PAT HUGHES ANNOUNCED WITH HARRY CARAY DURING THE 1996 AND 1997 CUBS' SEASONS.

This book/CD is all about Harry. You will hear his greatest play-by-play moments, from Stan Musial's 3,000th hit in 1958 to the famous Ryne Sandberg showdown with Bruce Sutter in 1984.

You will read about his sad childhood, his early days as a broadcaster, his rise to fame in St. Louis with the Cardinals in their 1964 championship season, some White Sox highlights, and the story of his Wrigley performances of "Take Me Out to the Ball Game."

You also will hear some of his funniest on-air moments. I dare you not to laugh out loud!

He was a legend in our business, and I am glad I got to know him a little bit. I hope you get to know him a little bit, too, as you read and listen!

Pat Hughes
April 2007

chapter 1

VOICE OF THE FANS

WHEN YOU THINK OF baseball in the twentieth century, certain names come quickly to mind: Babe Ruth, Walter Johnson, Joe DiMaggio, Mickey Mantle, Willie Mays, Hank Aaron, Cal Ripken, Ted Williams, Mel Allen, Ty Cobb, and Vin Scully. These are among the most recognizable players and broadcasters in baseball.

TRACK 1

HARRY'S FAMOUS CALLS AND "ONE OF THE FANS" ENTHUSIASM MADE HIM ONE OF THE MOST BELOVED BROADCASTERS IN HISTORY.

But without the fans—the paying public—there is no game.

Who represents the fan, the "everyman" who pays his way into the park, who tunes his radio to the local game or tries to pick up the faint, crackly signal of some far-away radio station?

In the twentieth century, perhaps no figure represented the fan as well as the great Harry Caray.

Using bully pulpits ranging from 50,000-watt radio station KMOX in St. Louis to Superstation WGN-TV in Chicago, Harry reached fans from coast to coast and brought them close to the game of baseball.

Sitting in his radio booth in St. Louis' Sportsman's Park and Busch Stadium, and from his TV and radio perches in Chicago's Comiskey Park and Wrigley Field, Harry preached the gospel of the pastime in living rooms, dens, and automobiles, and on front stoops and back porches throughout the nation, bringing images of Stan "The Man" Musial, Bob Gibson, Ken Boyer, Lou Brock, Dick Allen, Ryne Sandberg, and Sammy Sosa closer to the hearts of baseball-hungry fans from coast to coast.

Perhaps no other figure than the great Bambino himself, Babe Ruth, played so large a role in popularizing the game of baseball as Harry Caray.

Close your eyes and you can almost hear Harry now, bellowing, "Hello again, everybody, this is Harry Caray" as he got ready to bring you another afternoon or evening of baseball.

Much like a fan—and let's face it, he was the ultimate baseball fan—Harry took great pleasure in the game itself. In 53 years of broadcasting big-league baseball, Harry watched, enjoyed—really, you might say, ate and drank up—some 8,300 baseball games.

On any given warm summer day or night, you could find Harry perched in a broadcast booth or even seated in the bleachers, with a cooler of "cold ones" at his side. Harry spanned the technological ages. He was the chief reason the Cardinals were able to build a large regional radio network with KMOX Radio in St. Louis as its flagship. In his years with the Cubs, Harry was a national TV personality on Superstation WGN-TV.

Harry, no doubt, sold more beer, automobiles, and tickets to ball games than any other baseball announcer around.

How does one measure a broadcaster's love for the game? Well, even at age 80 and beyond, Harry would attend almost every spring-training game, even when he wasn't broadcasting. He'd go just to hang out, watch the game, be around the fans, coaches, and players. And of course, sing an impromptu version of "Take Me Out to the Ball Game" during the seventh-inning stretch. He absolutely loved the whole atmosphere of a ball game, even at spring-training.

When we debate the greatness of a broadcaster, it seems that every group of fans in every big-league market thinks their announcer is the best. It's impossible to say who is best. Fans in Pittsburgh loved Bob Prince and no doubt thought he was the best in the business. The same goes for Yankees fans, who adored Mel Allen, or Brooklyn Dodgers fans, who loved the folksy Red Barber. Fans of the Los Angeles Dodgers no doubt revere Vin Scully for his literary, melodious description of games. In Detroit, don't tell Tigers fans that anybody is better than Ernie Harwell.

But there is one argument that's hard to lose. Harry Caray probably was more loved by his fans than any broadcaster who ever lived. He had a stronger emotional bond. He was more their "spokesman" than any other broadcaster. All you had to experience was the Cubs bus pulling into town or Harry stepping out onto the catwalk of some park and hearing the fans yell, "Harry, Harry," when they saw him. In whatever party he was traveling with, Harry was the most recognizable figure—bigger, even, than the players.

Harry described his own situation as that of being a fan who somehow had gotten hold of a microphone and was able to broadcast games. Maybe it was because Harry had a way of saying, "Hello. Come on in. Come have a beer with me and enjoy this ball game for the next two or three hours. It's baseball. We're outside. How can you not have fun?"

Of course, Harry had the professional qualities that go into making a great broadcaster: the voice and the enthusiasm. He possessed great baseball knowledge and did his homework for every broadcast. If you measure the greatness of a broadcaster by qualities such as his home run call or the ability to rise to the occasion and make even the most mundane game sound exciting, Harry comes out on top. Throw in professionalism, longevity, sense of humor, and unique style, and there can be little argument that Harry had it all.

Just ask all the fans who love him.

chapter 2
THE 1984 CUBS

I T'S HARD TO IMAGINE baseball fans or a baseball announcer having more fun than Cubs fans and Harry Caray had in 1984.

TRACK 2

THREE YEARS INTO BROADCASTING FOR THE CUBS, HARRY COVERED A HISTORY-MAKING SEASON WITH FUTURE HALL-OF-FAMER RYNE SANDBERG.

Harry always told me his favorite Cubs team to cover was the 1984 team. No wonder. That season represented a turning point for the franchise: record attendance, a division championship, and Harry (then in his third season as the voice of the Cubs) happily singing "Take Me Out to the Ball Game" at Wrigley Field. One can make the argument that during the magical summer of 1984, the Cubs became "America's Team."

Picked by many to finish last or near last in the National League East, the Cubs did nothing to dispel those notions with a horrible spring-training record. But they wound up shocking the baseball world by winning their division and advancing to the post-season for the first time since 1945.

CUBS' RYNE SANDBERG LEAPS OVER PHILLIES' LEN MATUSZEK AS HE STEALS SECOND BASE.

Harry was there every step of the way to sing the Cubs' praises—literally. Who could forget Harry serenading catcher Jody Davis, with "Jo-Dee, Jo-Dee Davis," to the tune of "Davy Crockett"? Or how, whenever closer Lee Smith would nail down a save, or the "Red Baron," Rick Sutcliffe, would notch one of his 16 Cubs victories, Harry would bellow: "Cubs win! Cubs win! Cubs win!"

The signature moment of that magical summer of '84 came on June 23, a sunny Saturday at Wrigley Field, with the Cubs facing their Gateway Arch rivals, the St. Louis Cardinals. What took place that day was arguably the most famous game ever played at Wrigley Field, supplanting even Gabby Hartnett's 1938 "homer in the gloamin'."

Of the hundreds of thousands of baseball games played, very few bear the stamp of one individual. Of course, there was Bobby Thomson's "Shot Heard 'Round the World" in 1951 and Don Larsen's perfect game in the 1956 World Series.

The "Sandberg Game" was another, and Harry Caray was there to chronicle it.

With the Cubs down a run in the bottom of the ninth and facing seemingly invincible Cards closer Bruce Sutter, Sandberg launched a game-tying home run.

The Cardinals scored a pair in the top of the 10th, when Sandberg came up with a man on in the bottom of the inning, again facing Sutter.

Harry wasn't doing TV that day. The game was being televised by NBC as their Game of the Week, so Harry was working on WGN Radio. As you listen to his calls of both homers, you can feel the passion and energy in his 70-year-old voice. When he shouted, "There it goes!" for a second time, the legend of the "Sandberg Game" was born.

While on the Cubs annual winter caravan a few years ago, I had a chance to talk with Ryno about that special and memorable afternoon. I said, "How did you hit home runs against Sutter? Nobody was hitting

HARRY TALKING WITH CUBS' MANAGER JIM FREY BEFORE A BALL GAME.

homers against the guy." He said, "I knew he was going to throw that split-finger fastball. I knew he was going to throw it down low. I was looking for it, and I just kind of swung under it. I just lifted it. I knew he was going to throw it, but it was so good and such a devastating pitch that you knew it was coming but still had a hard time getting any elevation on it because it had such a late, sharp downward break. Somehow, I just kind of lifted it." As Ryne demonstrated it to me, he did so with a kind of golf swing.

It's incredibly rare for a closer to give up two homers in a game. And to the same hitter? I can't think of another time that's happened.

It is only a footnote that little-known utility man Dave Owen actually won the game with a single in the bottom of the 11th. This game forever will be known as Ryne Sandberg's official coming-out party.

After his joyous shouts of "Cubs win!" Harry's next words resonated, too: "I never saw a game like this in my life, and I've been around a long life. Holy cow! What a victory."

The true mark of Harry's professionalism was evident that day. Excited as he was about the two Sandberg homers and the Cubs victory, he remained in control, describing all the action without letting the emotion of the triumph overwhelm him.

The '84 Cubs season ended in major disappointment as they fell to the San

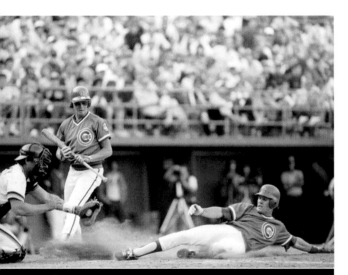

RYNE SANDBERG SLIDES IN TO HOME TO SCORE IN THE TOP OF THE 10TH INNING AGAINST SAN DIEGO.

Diego Padres in the National League Championship Series, losing three consecutive games in San Diego after handily taking the first two games at Wrigley. But it was still a memorable year, thanks to Ryne Sandberg and the miracle win over the Cardinals, Rick Sutcliffe, the "Daily Double" of leadoff man Bobby Dernier and Sandberg, Gary "Sarge" Matthews, and a division title.

Here is something unique to the Cubs. They didn't win it all in '84. They didn't win in '69. And yet, for the last 30–40 years, those are the two most popular teams the Chicago Cubs have had. The seasons of 1969 and 1984 captured the hearts of Chicago fans. Those summers were full of excitement and pathos. Maybe it has something to do with the long history of futility of the Cubs, or maybe it has something to do with the likability of the players of those teams.

And someone else also greatly assisted in the overall joy of 1984: Harry Caray.

HARRY AND RYNE IN 1996. HARRY COVERED RYNE SANDBERG'S ENTIRE BIG-LEAGUE CAREER WITH THE CUBS.

chapter 3

THE 1964 CARDINALS

IN ALL OF SPORTS, nothing quite matches the drama of the good, old-fashioned pennant race. Day after day, night after night, as the warm summer evenings give way to the cool autumn chill, baseball fans revel in the delicious agony of the standings. Suddenly, the long, 162-game season boils down to a test of wills, and fans hang on every pitch.

TRACK 3

HARRY COVERED THE 1964 PENNANT RACE WITH A LITTLE HELP FROM HIS FRIENDS, AND LONG-DISTANCE PHONE LINES.

The 1964 National League season produced a pennant race like no other, and Harry Caray was smack-dab in the middle of it. Remember, in 1964, divisions and playoffs were still five years away, and the wild card was thirty years off. There were ten teams in each league. Finish first, you play in the World Series. Finish anywhere else, you go home.

Harry's Cardinals hadn't been to the World Series since 1946. The

WHEN THE TEMPERATURE REACHED 100 DEGREES, HARRY SOMETIMES STRIPPED DOWN TO HIS BOXERS AND CARRIED ON BROADCASTING.

1964 team looked like it was going nowhere when the trading deadline of June 15 hit. On that date, the Cardinals obtained a speedy, but seemingly raw, outfielder from their archrivals, the Chicago Cubs, in exchange for veteran pitcher Ernie Broglio. The outfielder's name was Lou Brock.

LOU BROCK KNOCKS OVER YANKEES' PHIL LINZ TO BREAK UP A DOUBLE PLAY DURING THE 1964 WORLD SERIES.

Harry told me about a headline in a St. Louis paper that read, "Ernie Broglio for Who?" Well, Cardinals fans soon found out.

Harry, who'd turned 50 during spring training 1964, was preparing to work his 20th year as the voice of the Cardinals. As a broadcaster, you have a feeling sometimes how a season will go. At other times, you're completely surprised. One thing remains the same: you enter just about every baseball season with cheerful optimism, thinking,

"This could be the year."

Personally, I always hope for the best, prepare for the worst, try to stay loose, and be ready for anything. In listening to the CD track on the 1964 Cardinals, I chuckle when I hear Harry say, "The Cardinals are going to win this pennant" in only the third game of the year. But he was so surprised at pitcher Roger Craig's extra-base hit that he just blurted out the exclamation. Sometimes, you really do get a feeling early in the year, just the way things start to unfold, that this might be the year for your team.

Harry was an excellent radio man for several decades, and you hear him at his very best on this CD track. If your only memory of Harry is a gray-haired, grandfatherly figure at Wrigley Field singing, "Take Me Out to the Ball Game," you have experienced only a fraction of what made him great. It was his radio work, mainly with the Cardinals, that put him in the Hall of Fame.

For one thing, he could call a dramatic play as well as anyone who ever lived. The excitement in his voice was absolutely compelling. Remember, he grew up in St. Louis as a big Cardinals fan, so when he called a Redbirds game-winning hit, he was genuinely as happy as anyone listening.

Outside of Mike Shannon in St. Louis and Bob Uecker in Milwaukee, there aren't many big-league baseball broadcasters who spent more time in their hometown than Harry Caray and his 25-year run in St. Louis. Uecker, who has been broadcasting Brewers baseball for nearly four decades and is still going strong, was a catcher for the '64 Cardinals. Bob greatly admired Harry, once telling me, "Harry ruled St. Louis in those days. As a player, you tried to stay on his good side. If he got down on you, look out. Ken Boyer was the National League Most Valuable Player in 1964, but for some reason, he could never perform well enough to satisfy Harry Caray. Harry was as tough on Boyer as an announcer could possibly be. And the great majority of fans sided with Harry and not with Boyer or any other player. Harry was powerful, and he knew it."

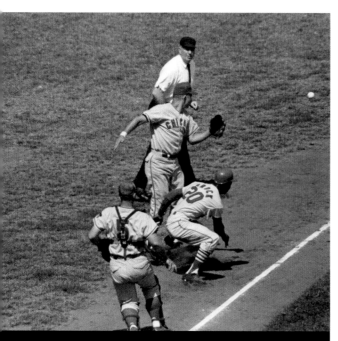

LOU BROCK SCORED AFTER BEING MOMENTARILY CAUGHT BETWEEN 3RD AND HOME BY THE CUBS.

The Cardinals owned a record of 28-31 on June 15, 1964, but Brock gave them a spark as he suddenly, almost magically, came into his own as a ballplayer. Brock had several skills that could help any team. He had blazing speed and could steal bases. He could hit for both average and power. He could lead off. Cubs' great Ron Santo still talks about Brock's homer into the distant center-field stands at New York's Polo Grounds. He's one of a very few to do that. Brock's fielding, although erratic at times, could be spectacular.

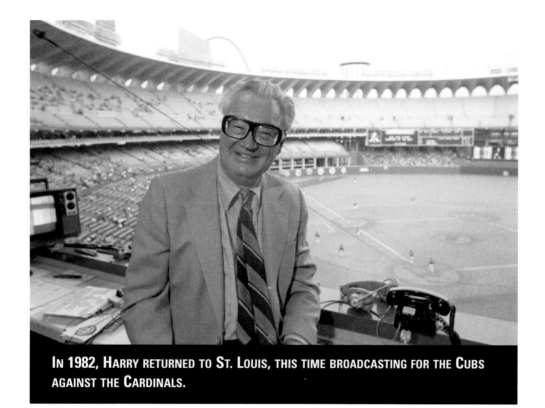

IN 1982, HARRY RETURNED TO ST. LOUIS, THIS TIME BROADCASTING FOR THE CUBS AGAINST THE CARDINALS.

Even though the Cardinals picked up steam after the acquisition of Brock, there seemed to be no stopping the Phillies, led by pitchers Jim Bunning and Chris Short, slugger Johnny Callison, and rookie sensation Richie Allen.

With 12 games left in the season, the Phils led the Cincinnati Reds by six and one-half games, with the Cardinals lurking.

All of a sudden, the Phillies fell into a 10-game losing streak from September 21 through September 30. Meanwhile, the Cardinals reeled off an eight-game winning streak from September 24 through September 30.

Harry could barely contain his excitement at the KMOX Radio microphone.

In 1964, most teams televised only a handful of games. There was no internet, no ESPN. Unless you were at the game, the radio play-by-play man was your witness to the team. Harry was in his element.

The excitement was electric as the season entered its final week. Harry went the extra mile to keep Cardinals fans throughout the vast

CARDINALS BOB GIBSON, KEN BOYER, AND TIM MCCARVER CELEBRATE AFTER DEFEATING THE YANKEES TO WIN THE 1964 WORLD SERIES.

KMOX listening area up-to-date on the epic pennant race.

Harry could seem to be in two places at once. When the Cardinals won their final Tuesday game of the season, he shouted, "Cardinals win it." Just seconds later, with one eye on the scoreboard, Harry let Cardinals fans in on more good news: "Pittsburgh has won...The National League race is in a tie....Holy cow! Never has there been a more thrilling moment!"

Was he overstating? Perhaps just a bit, but that line tells you what the moment meant to Harry.

Harry displayed both his work ethic and his grasp of history during that final week of the '64 season. After the Cardinals had beat the Phillies one night, Harry stayed on air long after Busch Stadium was empty, waiting for the outcome of the Pirates–Reds game that would determine whether the Cards were alone in first place, or shared it with the Reds. Harry called Jim Woods, a Pirates radio announcer, on the telephone, and Woods relayed the Pirates game to Harry.

"Hey-hey!" Harry shouted when Woods informed him the Cardinals were alone in first place.

When the Cardinals clinched on the final day of the season, averting a season-ending sweep at the hands of the lowly New York Mets, Harry was down on the field for the final out.

"The Cardinals win the pennant, the Cardinals win the pennant, the Cardinals win the pennant!" Harry shouted before joining the fray on the field.

So, in 1964, Harry was as excited as he could possibly be—and as good as he could possibly be, especially as the pennant race surged to the finish line.

chapter 4

HARRY'S CHILDHOOD

W HO COULD NOT SMILE upon hearing Harry's famous greeting, "Hello again, everybody, this is Harry Caray. It's a beautiful day for baseball!" Those uplifting words signaled that, for a couple of hours at least, you could set aside your cares and enjoy an afternoon or evening of baseball. One of Harry's greatest gifts was the ability to bring a smile to the faces of fans young and old.

TRACK 4

HEAR THE STORY OF HARRY'S EARLY DAYS IN ST. LOUIS, AND HOW HE FIRST FELL IN LOVE WITH BASEBALL.

But it's a sad irony that Harry's childhood was anything but uplifting, and it's a tribute to his persistence and work ethic that he didn't let this get the best of him.

Harry Caray was born Harry Christopher Carabina in St. Louis, Missouri. There's some question as to the exact date of Harry's birth, but it's believed to be March 1, 1914.

Harry's childhood was anything but easy or pleasant. He had no

(ABOVE) HARRY'S FATHER, CHRIS CARABINA (BELOW) HARRY WITH HIS SON, SKIP, WHO FOLLOWED HARRY'S FOOTSTEPS INTO BROADCASTING

memory of his father, Chris Carabina, whom he never met. His mother died when he was seven years old, so Harry went to live with his mother's brother. When the uncle disappeared, Harry was raised by the man's wife, Doxie Argint, who provided the young man with some sense of family and stability.

Because of his lonely and difficult childhood, Christmastime was always sad and melancholy for Harry, even well into his old age. He often told friends that the tears would roll down his face on Christmas morning as his thoughts turned to his own childhood. It wasn't until very late in life, when he was in the company of his grandchildren, that Harry was able to enjoy the holiday as he doled out presents to the kids.

Harry's youth was hard-scrabble. Growing up in a tough environment in St. Louis, the equally tough youngster made the best of it. He became an avid reader, a skill that would serve him well the rest of his life in his chosen profession. He developed a strong vocabulary, command of the language, and the ability to communicate in a robust way.

All the while, Harry took various jobs to earn pocket money. He sold newspapers at the age of eight. He later tended bar and took a job as a salesman for a manufacturing company. But his first love was baseball, and he became an avid fan of the St. Louis Cardinals, further laying the foundation for his career.

If there is a seminal moment in Harry's professional life, it came when listening to Cardinals radio broadcasts and realizing he could describe the games with more energy and excitement than the play-by-play announcer. He sent a letter to the general manager of KMOX Radio in St. Louis, a powerful station that later would bill itself as the "Voice of St. Louis."

Cocky? Perhaps, but few people go places in this world without some measure of self-confidence, and history has proved Harry right.

The station manager helped Harry land his first job in radio in Joliet, Illinois. The first step of a long and memorable journey was under way.

chapter 5

JOLIET AND KALAMAZOO

ASK ANY MEDIA PERSON, whether a broadcaster or a writer, and almost all will tell you they started small. Perhaps it was at the high school or college newspaper or radio station. Or maybe at a weekly paper, covering high school football games on rainy Friday nights or at a low-watt radio station calling basketball games by night or reading the farm reports by sunrise.

TRACK 5

HARRY STARTED HIS CAREER ANNOUNCING BAS-KETBALL AND FOOTBALL, EVENTUALLY CALLING THE 1960 COTTON BOWL FEATURING FUTURE HEISMAN TROPHY WINNER ERNIE DAVIS.

As big a star as Harry Caray became, he too paid his dues by working his way up the broadcasting ladder. Harry began seriously honing his craft at radio station WCLS in Joliet, Illinois, about 50 miles southwest of Chicago.

Although we think of Harry primarily as a baseball announcer, he began by calling the play-by-play of high school football and basketball games. Later, he would also gain his share of acclaim working St. Louis Hawks basketball games in the NBA and University of Missouri college

HARRY WITH HIS SON, SKIP, IN JOLIET

football. He often said one of his greatest thrills was broadcasting the Missouri Tigers' upset of college football powerhouse Notre Dame.

And Harry's call of the 1960 Cotton Bowl game between top-ranked Syracuse University and the No. 2-ranked University of Texas demonstrated just how versatile and skilled a broadcaster Harry was, especially in setting a scene and crisply describing even the most complex football plays as they unfolded.

That kind of skill was developed in Joliet and at Harry's second job, that of sports director at WKZO Radio in Kalamazoo, Michigan. That station claims two broadcasting legends: Harry Caray and the great radio newscaster Paul Harvey. Imagine the odds of two broadcasting giants crossing paths early on at the same small station.

One summer, a little later on, WKZO sent Harry down the road to Battle Creek, Michigan, where something very important developed during a semi-pro baseball game. During the game, Harry first began using a home run call that became famous from coast to coast: "It might be...it could be...it IS! A home run!" Then, Harry might punctuate that home run call with: "Holy cow!"

"Holy cow" became Harry's signature exclamation, and he cheerfully bellowed it for a half-century.

Although former Yankees shortstop and broadcaster Phil Rizzuto claimed "Holy cow" as his own, Harry correctly pointed out that he was using the phrase while "The Scooter" was still cavorting on the ballfield for the Yankees.

IN 1940 HARRY BEGAN HIS FIRST RADIO JOB CONDUCTING "MAN ON THE STREET" INTERVIEWS.

Harry's cries of "It might be...it could be...it IS!" and "Holy cow!" developed in the best way: spontaneously. Many broadcasters today fret long and hard about developing a home run call. The pure magic of "Holy cow!" was that Harry didn't need to think about it or try it out or contrive it. It just came out one day, unrehearsed. Over the years, Harry's listeners could almost anticipate its exact arrival. It was sure to follow Harry's

home run call, but often came on a great defensive play, such as: "Flood on the run, on the run, on the run...sensational catch...holy cow!"

Even in those early days, Harry Caray sounded like no other broadcaster. This was no cookie-cutter announcer in the making. Armed with experience, a couple of signature calls, and a style all his own, Harry was ready for the big time.

"IT'S A BEAUTIFUL DAY FOR A BALL GAME."

chapter 6

CARDINALS RADIO

HARRY CARAY'S FIRST announcing partner in the major leagues was Gabby Street. Harry adored Gabby, a former player and manager who taught Harry a great deal about the game: how a pitcher worked a batter, the strategy of the game, when to bunt, when to swing away, when to make a pitching change, and when to steal a base.

TRACK 6

HARRY LOVED THE CARDINALS, COVERING THEIR THREE NATIONAL LEAGUE PENNANT RACES DURING THE 1960s.

More important, Gabby was a real father figure to Harry, something Harry had missed as a child. The chemistry clicked immediately.

Before all Cardinals games were broadcast live, Harry and Gabby did numerous "re-creations" of road games. In the 1946 pennant race, Harry's work on those re-creations really established him in St. Louis. The re-creations involved Harry in a St. Louis studio receiving Western Union ticker information from wherever the Cardinals were playing. Harry would then "re-create" the play-by-play for his listeners. In doing

GABBY STREET, WHO WOULD BECOME HARRY'S PARTNER BROADCASTING FOR THE CARDINALS IN THE 1940S AND 1950S, MANAGED THE CARDINALS TO A WORLD SERIES VICTORY IN 1931.

so, he displayed his many talents —his imagination, his creativity, his gift of gab, and his love for baseball.

In the 1940s, there weren't as many exclusive arrangements between teams and radio stations as there are today. Several stations might all broadcast the same game. In Chicago at one time you could listen to five different radio stations broadcasting Cubs games at the same moment.

In 1947, Harry and Gabby Street were chosen to be the St. Louis Cardinals voices for all 154 games, both home and away.

KMOX in St. Louis became the Cardinals flagship station in 1953. Thanks mainly to Harry Caray, KMOX would build a vast network of more than 200 stations, spanning the Midwest and extending out toward the West Coast.

Each time a new station joined the network in, say, Montana or New Mexico, those listeners were getting their first taste of baseball on the radio. Therefore, Harry Caray was their first link to our national pastime.

Harry became an absolute legend in St. Louis. He brought the game to life on the radio. He could make a dull game sound good and a good game sound great.

The 1950s Cardinals did not win any National League pennants, but they featured one of baseball's greatest all-time hitters: Stan "The Man" Musial. Musial once cracked five homers in a 1954 doubleheader

IN 1954, JACK BUCK BECAME HARRY'S PARTNER. THEY CONTINUED ANNOUNCING TOGETHER UNTIL HARRY LEFT THE CARDINALS IN 1969.

against the Giants. That's one of the biggest days a big-leaguer has ever had.

Harry told me one of his biggest broadcasting thrills came in May of 1958, the day Musial collected his 3,000th hit at Chicago's Wrigley Field. It was the final day of a road trip. The Cardinals had planned to wait until they got back to St. Louis to let Stan the Man reach the milestone in front of the hometown folks. But the Cardinals and Cubs were locked in a tight duel, and Stan, pinch-hitting late in the game against Moe Drabowsky, cracked an opposite-field double to left for base hit No. 3,000. Harry Caray captured the moment beautifully.

As you listen to his call of hit No. 3,000, you'll hear his excitement and the admiration in his voice for Stan the Man. In moments like these, as an announcer, you almost have to tell yourself to pull back a little bit. You know you're going to get excited about a milestone. Everyone in the park is excited. But if you get too fired up and too excited, you might not make the call you want to make, or the one, a year later, you wished you'd made. Milestones can be tricky because you know they're coming

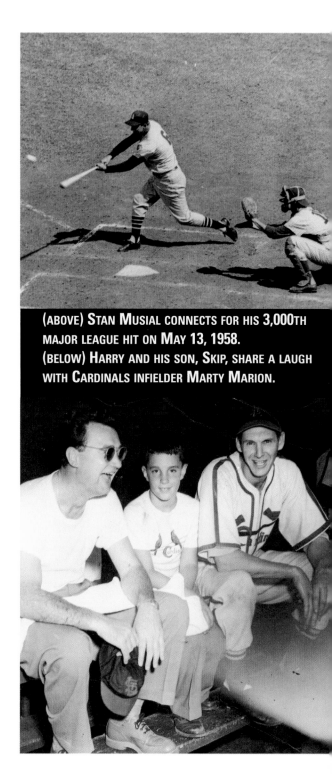

(ABOVE) STAN MUSIAL CONNECTS FOR HIS 3,000TH MAJOR LEAGUE HIT ON MAY 13, 1958. (BELOW) HARRY AND HIS SON, SKIP, SHARE A LAUGH WITH CARDINALS INFIELDER MARTY MARION.

at you—unlike, say, a triple play or a sensational catch that just surprises you out of the blue.

HARRY INTERVIEWING CARDINALS MANAGER HARRY WALKER IN THE DUGOUT AT BUSCH STADIUM BEFORE A DOUBLE-HEADER AGAINST THE CUBS.

Harry could really rise to the moment and deliver the big call. Invariably, he was under control and easy to understand regardless of his excitement.

After Gabby Street died, Jack Buck joined Harry in 1954. Joe Garagiola joined the announcing crew the next season. Not a bad local

RT FLOOD, ROGER MARIS, ORLANDO CEPEDA, AND LOU BROCK, SHOWN RE AT WRIGLEY FIELD BEFORE A 1967 OUTING AGAINST THE CUBS, WERE NSIDERED THE CARDINALS' "BIG BATS" THAT SEASON.

radio team, I would say, considering all three ended up in Cooperstown in the broadcasters' wing of the Baseball Hall of Fame.

But Harry Caray was the dominant voice and personality of Cardinals radio for a quarter-century. In fact, Caray and Buck would become one of the most legendary radio broadcast teams in big-league history. Great ball clubs assist in creating great broadcasters, and the 1960s Cardinals made Harry and Jack larger than life. It's hard to identify another pair who can be considered on par with Harry and Jack. Although there have been other announcing teams who have enjoyed immense popularity over the years, I'll take Harry Caray and Jack Buck on Cardinals radio and TV in the 1960s as the best team ever.

chapter 7

SHOW BUSINESS
AND FUN

BASEBALL ISN'T A MATTER of life or death. It only seems that way to the players and fans.

As much as Harry Caray lived and died with the Cardinals, White Sox, and Cubs, he knew baseball and sports were, at their core, for fun. He also knew they were show biz. And as a showman, Harry Caray had few rivals in the baseball broadcast booth.

TRACK 7

HARRY KNEW HE WAS NOT JUST A BROADCASTER BUT AN ENTERTAINER PLAYING TO THE CROWD. HE WOULD KID AROUND WITH HIS BROADCAST PART-NERS AND HAVE FUN WITH PLAYERS' NAMES TO KEEP THINGS LIVELY.

Harry was one of the first baseball announcers to inject an element of show business into his broadcasts. He seemed to sense that fans wanted to be both informed and entertained. Before his career began, when he would listen to other announcers, he'd think they sounded dull. He knew he could be much more stimulating than most of them—and he was.

He realized his job wasn't simply calling balls and strikes and outs. He always tried to spice things up with humor, storytelling, vocal inflec-tions, laughter, and, at times, just plain outrageousness. Even well past his 80th birthday, he loved to tell stories that made you laugh, always with a mischievous twinkle in his eye. As you listened, you knew there was some embellishment to his yarns, but you didn't care.

HARRY TAKES A SWING, JOINING THE CARDINALS DURING BATTING PRACTICE.

Harry's love for the teams he covered was genuine. And that genuine love translated into some of the most entertaining baseball announcing ever on both radio and television.

Whenever Harry's team was in trouble or faced a tense situation, you could count on Harry to warn: "There's danger here, Cherie." Now, we're not quite sure who "Cherie" was, but we do know she was duly warned of the danger.

Of course, no Harry Caray baseball broadcast would be complete without Harry letting us know that it was "A beautiful day for baseball."

After an exciting play, you could sense an imminent "Holy cow!"

There were other Harry standards. If he was particularly dismayed by his team's play, he'd roll out a "Boy, oh, boy," as in, "Boy, oh, boy, we can't get anybody out."

If a local hero failed in the clutch, you could hear the pain in Harry's voice when he moaned, "Poppppped it up."

Harry's flair for the dramatic was legendary. In November 1968, he was struck by an automobile in St. Louis and nearly killed. Months of rehab carried into the following spring, and Harry was almost 100 percent, but that didn't stop him from making the most of the situation to bring down the house on Opening Day at Busch Stadium in 1969.

Because of his remarkable comeback, the Cardinals decided to introduce Harry before the game. Feebly coming out of the Cardinals dugout on a pair of canes, Harry suddenly stopped and flung one of them as far as he could. Naturally, the Busch Stadium

HARRY TRIES TO INTERVIEW WALLY MOON (LEFT), WHILE HERMAN WEHMEIER (CENTER) AND EDDIE KASKO (RIGHT) DISTRACT HIM.

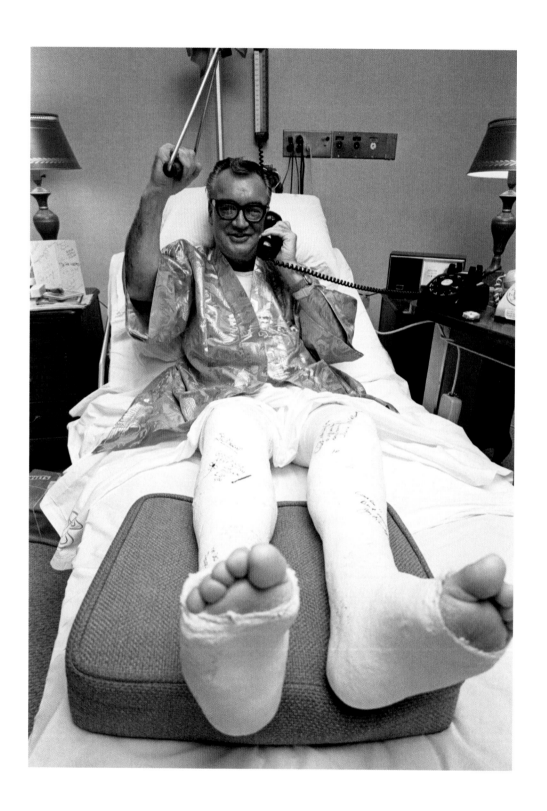

crowd ate it up. A few steps later, he flung the other one. The joint went up for grabs.

When he got back to the dugout, Harry was greeted by Cardinals pitcher Bob Gibson, who knew exactly what Harry was up to with this preposterous stunt. Gibson looked at Harry and told him he knew full well Harry didn't need those canes—that they were only props. Harry looked at him and said, "This is show business."

That story sums up Harry at his best.

Harry loved to spell names backward and pronounce them on the air. One of his favorites was Tigers catcher John Wockenfuss. "Wockenfuss spelled backwards is 'Ssufnekcow,'" Harry would say before chuckling, "Boy, oh, boy, that sounds a lot like 'Holy cow.'" Harry had all kinds of fun spelling Mark Grudzielanek and Jason Isringhausen backward. If there was a guy with a palindrome for a last name, such as Dave Otto, Robb Nen, Mark Salas, or Toby Harrah, Harry was all over it.

Sometimes when I was working with him on a broadcast, I would walk into the booth and find Harry doing some "homework" on the game. I'd say, "Hi, Harry, how are you doing?" He'd say, "Fine, Pat, I'm just spelling all the ballplayers' names back-

SAMMY SOSA BLOWS A KISS AFTER HITTING A HOMER.

(ABOVE) HARRY WITH JACK BUCK, BROADCASTING FROM THE STANDS.
(BELOW) LOU BROCK DIVES SAFELY HOME DURING THE 1967 WORLD SERIES AGAINST THE RED SOX.

wards and seeing if I could pronounce them."

Harry had all kinds of fun with names, some of it intentional and some of it not. You could never be sure. When Ryne Sandberg, Jim Sundberg, and Scott Sanderson all were on the field at the same time for the Cubs, Harry mixed and matched their names to seemingly every mathematical possibility, from Sanderberg to Sunderson to Ryneberg.

Harry knew a showman on the field when he saw one, too. When the Cubs acquired colorful Sammy Sosa from the White Sox in 1992, Harry knew the Cubs had something special, years before Sammy made history with his home runs.

During Cubs telecasts, Harry would exhort legendary WGN-TV producer-director Arne Harris with: "Arne, get the camera on Sammy!" Arne would oblige, and viewers would see Sammy blowing kisses to the fans, racing out to right field, or tapping his heart and blowing a kiss to his mom.

Harry didn't mind that the cameras occasionally revealed a little vulnerability in his veneer, either. There was the time when Harry sat on the "cough button," thus cutting off the sound for several minutes as he looked into the camera and talked. Another time, he got a teabag stuck between his headset and glasses and went on the air with the teabag dangling along the side of his face. No doubt that brought a hearty guffaw from Harry once his crew informed him what had happened.

And I dare you to keep a straight face as you listen to the segment with Harry, Ron Santo, and Thom Brennaman on Cubs radio circa 1993 as the three joke about Ronny's hairpiece. It's absolutely one of the funniest things I've ever heard on a baseball broadcast. Harry is laughing uncontrollably while attempting to do the play-by-play.

Late in his life, Harry just seemed to make having fun on the air one of his highest priorities. If he made mistakes and got confused, he didn't care. He knew the audience was having fun right along with him, and that's what Harry was all about.

Sometimes he was funny when he wasn't even trying to be humorous. One time on camera he grabbed what he thought was a microphone and started speaking into it. Trouble was, it wasn't a mike, but a gooseneck lamp. He was announcing into a lamp for a couple of minutes.

I always remember him telling me to have fun with the game, especially when the team was not winning.

From dancing to "Rock Around the Clock" for the fans at Comiskey

IN 1994, HILLARY CLINTON VISITED HARRY IN THE CUBS' BOOTH. HARRY GAVE HER A WARM WELCOME.

Park or helping Arne Harris find one of his famous "hat shots" at Wrigley Field, Harry knew baseball was much more than a game.

It was a stage, and he played it for all it was worth.

chapter 8

OAKLAND

IT SHOULD HAVE BEEN a match made in heaven: Harry Caray and Charles O. Finley. After all, these were two of the biggest and most flamboyant promoters of baseball of their time. Charlie Finley, an insurance magnate from Chicago, was an innovator far ahead of his time. He moved the Athletics from Kansas City to Oakland for the start of the 1968 season, hoping to capitalize on the growing market the San Francisco Bay Area provided.

TRACK 8

HARRY WORKED IN OAKLAND FOR ONE SEASON BEFORE MOVING TO CHICAGO, WHERE HE WOULD SPEND THE REST OF HIS CAREER.

The Cardinals had let Harry go at the end of the 1969 season, and Harry hooked on with Charlie Finley's Oakland Athletics in 1970. The reputation Harry had built for himself in the game was legendary. He not only was the voice of the Cardinals, but that of the greater heartland and the common man.

Both Charlie Finley and Harry Caray had a knack for showmanship and for promoting the game of baseball. But Harry's one season in the

OAKLAND'S ROLLIE FINGERS, ONE OF THE FIRST PERMANENT RELIEF PITCHERS, WOULD LATER BE NAMED A WORLD SERIES MVP AND WIN THE CY YOUNG AWARD.

CATFISH HUNTER (ABOVE) AND VIDA BLUE (BELOW) LED THE A'S TO A SECOND-PLACE FINISH IN 1970. THE FOLLOWING YEAR WOULD SEE THE A'S TAKE THE AL WEST DIVISION BUT LOSE TO BALTIMORE IN THE PLAYOFFS.

Bay Area was largely uneventful.

Although Harry's impact was not as great as Charlie Finley had anticipated, during his one season in Oakland Harry rediscovered or had it reaffirmed for him that he loved baseball and loved being around the game. He loved the strategy. He loved the big moments in a ball game for a broadcaster. That was the important thing.

The A's, however, fought an uphill battle for the public's attention in the Bay Area, despite a roster that included Reggie Jackson, Vida Blue, and other future stars. Being the new kids on the block in the Bay Area, the A's had to share the spotlight with the firmly established San Francisco Giants. Even during their glory years, the A's often played before seas of empty seats in the vast Oakland-Alameda County Coliseum.

Whether Harry left the A's on his own or whether the often-meddlesome and heavy-handed Charlie Finley pushed him out after one season is still open to speculation. In the end, Harry's short stay in the

Bay Area remains a footnote—maybe even an obscure answer to a trivia question—in a long and glorious career.

HARRY LAUGHS WITH WHITE SOX MANAGER CHUCK TANNER DURING A 1974 PRESS CALL.

chapter 9

WHITE SOX

I F EVER A TEAM needed a jolt of excitement, it was the 1971 Chicago White Sox. The 1970 squad compiled a record of 56-106 and played in a near-empty Comiskey Park, then known as White Sox Park. In 1970, the White Sox drew just 495,355 fans for their entire season of home games.

TRACK 9

AT COMISKEY PARK, HARRY WOULD OCCASIONALLY BROADCAST FROM THE STANDS, SHIRTLESS, WITH A CASE OF BEER.

Team owner John Allyn, who had taken over the team from his brother Arthur a couple of years earlier, hired Harry Caray to be the Sox' new radio announcer for 1971.

Harry was quite a contrast from the legendary Bob Elson, whose somnambulant tones were thought to be out of touch in a fast-paced world in which football was emerging as the most exciting spectator sport.

There was work to do on the South Side of Chicago, both on and off the field. The biggest problem facing the White Sox and Harry in 1971 was the lack of a Chicago radio station. After three straight losing seasons and lagging fan interest, no big Chicago station wanted the Sox. So the Sox worked out a deal with suburban station WTAQ of LaGrange, whose signal, in some parts of the city, often came through as static.

Nevertheless, Harry gave it an enthusiastic go. With new manager Chuck Tanner, the Sox swept an opening-day doubleheader in Oakland before coming home to 43,253 fans for a Good Friday home opener at Comiskey. The Sox won their home opener over the Twins, stumbled for a stretch and then surged at the end of the season, signaling better times to come.

Armed with an attendance clause in his contract, Harry talked up the Sox as never before, and he pocketed a $20,000 bonus as home attendance swelled to 833,891.

Harry began broadcasting a few games from the center-field bleachers that year, armed with his fishing net (for snagging 440-foot home runs) and his cooler full of beer.

DICK ALLEN SLIDES HOME, BUT IS LATE: YANKEES CATCHER THURMAN MUNSON IS WAITING WITH THE BALL.

In 1972, the Sox battled the Oakland A's for the American League West title before falling out of the race at the end of the season. During a crucial game in Oakland in August, Harry's call on radio was the only available access—the Sox didn't regularly televise from the West Coast in those days.

When Ed Spiezio hit the game-winning homer, Harry's call of "Holy cow!" and "Sox win!" echoed from transistor radios across the city.

The Sox added a major attraction in '72. Dick Allen hit a team-record 37 homers, winning the MVP award in the American League.

Harry insisted on calling Allen by his old nickname "Richie," and his

cry of "There it goes, it might be, it could be, it is, a tremendous home run by Richie Allen. Holy cow!" energized the Sox fans.

Harry put the Sox back on 50,000-watt WMAQ Radio in 1973, when he took over TV duties as well. But the Sox slid back in the standings, and by 1975, owner Allyn was looking to sell.

Allyn was growing weary of Harry's criticisms of the team, and Harry had made an enemy of Sox third baseman Bill Melton, who as recently as 1971 had won the American League home run title. Whenever Melton would pop out, Harry would groan, "Popppped it up, that wouldn't be a home run in a phone booth."

Before Allyn sold the team to Bill Veeck, he went on the local CBS TV station and told sportscaster Johnny Morris that Harry wouldn't be back. Legend has it that Harry ran into Allyn at a restaurant, flipped him a dime and said, "Next time you want to fire me, give me a call."

But, as it turned out, Veeck and Harry were made for each other. Both loved baseball, the common man—and their suds.

The 1976 Sox weren't much on the field, but Veeck's zany promotions (Greek Night came replete with belly dancers on the field, and the

Sox even wore shorts for one game of a doubleheader) and Harry's broadcasts kept things interesting, to say the least.

The 1977 Sox, a.k.a. the South Side Hitmen, provided new excite-

COMISKEY PARK WAS THE HOME OF THE CHICAGO WHITE SOX FROM 1910 TO 1990.

ment on the field with the likes of sluggers Oscar Gamble and Richie Zisk. Harry had a new broadcast partner, too: the irrepressible Jimmy Piersall, the former standout center fielder. Harry and Jimmy clicked instantly. They were pointed, funny, irreverent, and not to be missed.

The Harry-Jimmy show lasted through 1981. The year before, Veeck sold the White Sox to a group headed by investment guru Jerry Reinsdorf and TV mogul Eddie Einhorn. Under Veeck, Comiskey Park had become known as the world's largest outdoor beer garden . Reinsdorf and Einhorn wanted to change the Sox' image and make Comiskey Park more "family friendly."

By 1982, the new Sox owners were looking to restrict over-the-air TV broadcasts in favor of a pay-TV outlet. Harry, who never was enamored of the new owners, knew this would cut his exposure dramatically.

A new home awaited on the North Side of Chicago.

(ABOVE) HARRY STANDS BETWEEN SOX GENERAL MANAGER STU HOLCOMB AND OWNER JOHN ALLYN AT THE ANNOUNCEMENT THAT HARRY WOULD ANNOUNCE THE SOX ON TV IN 1973.
(BELOW) IN 1977 THE WHITE SOX ADDED MARY SHANE, A SPORTSCASTER FROM MILWAUKEE, TO THE BOOTH FOR 20 HOME GAMES.

chapter 10

TAKE ME OUT TO THE BALL GAME

EVERY BASEBALL FAN knows the words:

Take me out to the ball game,

Take me out with the crowd.

Buy me some peanuts and Cracker Jack,

I don't care if I never get back,

Let me root, root, root for the home team,

If they don't win it's a shame.

For it's one, two, three strikes, you're out

At the old ball game.

TRACK 10

HARRY SANG "TAKE ME OUT TO THE BALL GAME" FOR TWENTY YEARS, STARTING EACH 7TH INNING STRETCH WITH "A-ONE, A-TWO, A-THREE…" WHILE THE CROWD JOINED IN.

Those lyrics are from a song penned by Jack Norworth in 1908. It's said Mr. Norworth wrote the song on a piece of scrap paper while riding a train bound for New York.

"Take Me Out to the Ball Game" is as important a part of the

American baseball experience as home runs, hot dogs, and, well, peanuts and Cracker Jack.

The song has endured many decades, but nobody did more to popularize this paean to baseball than Harry Caray. Harry always loved

singing the song, but it was about midway through his tenure with the White Sox that it became a Chicago institution, one that accompanied both Chicago teams wherever they went.

Colorful showman Bill Veeck bought the White Sox in late 1975. During the 1976 season, the ever-observant Veeck noticed that Harry would rise with the crowd during the seventh inning stretch and sing "Take Me Out to the Ball Game." The Sox fans adored Harry, and all eyes were on the TV booth during the stretch.

Veeck got the idea to secretly install a public-address microphone into the booth so that Harry's voice would boom out over the Comiskey Park loudspeakers.

Thus a tradition was born. Veeck told Harry that his singing voice was so bad that

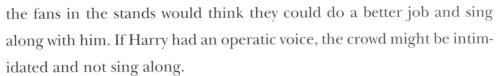

the fans in the stands would think they could do a better job and sing along with him. If Harry had an operatic voice, the crowd might be intimidated and not sing along.

From 1976–81, Harry would rise from his perch in the TV booth and implore Comiskey Park organist Nancy Faust to join him. "Root, root, root for the home team," of course, became, "Root, root, root for the White Sox."

STARTING IN 1998, SPECIAL "GUEST CONDUCTORS" WOULD SING "TAKE ME OUT TO THE BALL GAME" AT WRIGLEY FIELD, INCLUDING BOZO THE CLOWN

The tradition became so popular that Harry and several thousand loyal Sox fans carried it with them to Milwaukee's County Stadium. Brewers' owner and future Commissioner of Baseball Bud Selig wasn't happy about the Sox and their boisterous fans taking over his ballpark, and he nixed the idea of allowing Harry to use the public-address system.

No matter. Harry and the fans sang a capella.

The big question in Chicago was what would happen to the seventh-inning tradition when Harry moved from the White Sox to the Cubs for the 1982 season. Silly question. With a couple of modifications, the tradition moved from the South Side to the North Side.

Harry began his Wrigley Field rendition with, "Ah, one, ah, two, ah, three." And of course, he was now root, root, rooting for the Cubbies.

The tradition became an instant hit at Wrigley Field. No matter what the score, no matter if the beloved home team was winning or getting blown out, nobody left the ballpark until they joined Harry. If the Cubs were losing big, fans would wait to make a mass exodus after Harry sang, just as if a visiting player had crushed a bases-clearing double.

Such a simple song. Such simple fun. It was baseball. It was Harry Caray. And it was all about the fans.

Ernie Harwell, the Hall of Fame announcer of the Detroit Tigers whose own voice bore a trademark southern lilt, wondered aloud: "Why didn't I think of that way back when?"

Even after Harry's death, the tradition lived on at Wrigley Field. Shortly after Harry died, Cubs marketing and broadcasting chief John McDonough came up with the idea of continuing the seventh-inning stretch tradition to honor Harry, but with a twist. McDonough's idea was to employ a "guest conductor."

The first guest conductor, fittingly enough, was Harry's beloved wife, Dutchie. Her rendition on Opening Day 1998 brought the house down, along with her warm embrace of Harry's successor in the booth, grandson Chip Caray.

JIMMY BUFFETT TAKES A DAY OFF FROM MARGARITAVILLE TO SING AT WRIGLEY FIELD.

Since then, the guest conductor program has been a rousing success, even when the singers struggle with the words or the melody, or even the venue.

Who can forget former Chicago Bears coach Mike Ditka barely making it on time and rushing through the lyrics? And how about NASCAR driver Jeff Gordon referring to the Cubs cathedral as "Wrigley Stadium"?

The seventh-inning stretch at Wrigley Field has taken on a life of its own. The Cubs receive countless requests each year from agents, producers, and PR specialists attempting to gain some exposure for their clients.

I personally have met many famous people in the process. Before they sing in the seventh, they almost always stop by our WGN Radio booth in the sixth to visit with Ron Santo and me.

The great Jimmy Buffett has visited four or five times over the past decade, and I have loved his music for 35 years or more. Other luminaries who have stopped by include Shania Twain, Bill Murray, Mel Gibson, Ann-Margret, Jerry Lewis, Kenny Rogers (the singer, not the pitcher), Chuck Berry, Toby Keith, and the members of the band Chicago, just to name a few.

To this day, even though Harry has been gone for years, Cubs fans everywhere can be heard singing "Take Me Out to the Ball Game" and root, root, rooting for the Cubbies wherever they are, whether it be spring training, at home, or on the road.

Thanks, Harry.

chapter 11

THE CUBS

HARRY CARAY SHOCKED the Chicago public in November of 1981 when he jumped from the White Sox to the Cubs for the 1982 baseball season.

For Sox fans, this was tantamount to treason.

Cubs fans wanted to know how this long-time icon of the South Side would adapt to the North Side. After all, in Chicago, you're either a Cubs fan or a White Sox fan. For most, there is no middle ground.

Yet, from Opening Day 1982, when Harry took the microphone for his first Cubs game at Cincinnati's Riverfront Stadium, the fit was as natural as can be. Harry's love of baseball transcended all else, and when the Cubs did well, he rejoiced. When they failed—as they did much of the time in '82 and '83—Harry suffered right along with the fans.

Before long, Cubs fans took to Harry. They loved his passion and

TRACK 11

WITHIN A COUPLE OF SEASONS AT WRIGLEY FIELD, IT SEEMED LIKE HARRY HAD BEEN WITH THE CUBS FOREVER. HIS SHOUTS OF "CUBS WIN! CUBS WIN!" QUICKLY BECAME PART OF LIFE ON THE NORTH SIDE.

CUBS SCORE IN '85: RON CEY (ABOVE) IS WELCOMED AT HOME PLATE BY LEON DURHAM AFTER HITTING A THREE-RUN HOMER AGAINST THE PIRATES.
JODY DAVIS (BELOW) SCORES WHILE EXPOS' CATCHER MIKE FITZGERALD WAITS FOR THE BALL.

enthusiasm for the game, and Wrigley Field provided the perfect backdrop for such Harry-isms as "It's a beautiful day for a ball game" and "You can't beat fun at the old ballpark."

When Dallas Green took over as Cubs president and general manager for the 1982 season, he talked of "building a new tradition." Harry Caray was a key player of that new tradition.

Harry brought with him his seventh-inning-stretch rendition of "Take Me Out to the Ball Game." Just as fans did at Comiskey Park, fans would turn toward the booth and shout, "Harry, Harry," and Harry would respond with a smile, a wave, and maybe a salute with his beverage cup.

During his time in the Cubs' TV booth, from 1982–97, Harry teamed with analyst Steve Stone. The two became immensely popular. Often, they'd bicker like an old married couple, such as when Steve's cigar smoke would overwhelm Harry or if they disagreed on one of the finer points of baseball. But Harry

respected the baseball player in Steve, and Steve respected the professionalism and the announcer in Harry.

More often than not, they provided entertaining TV, with Harry calling it like the fan he was and Steve providing sharp, often prescient, commentary and analysis. And if Harry mispronounced a few names along the way, such as "Rafael Palermo" instead of Palmeiro or "Gordon McRae" for Brian McRae, what was the harm?

For a time, Harry shuttled between the TV and radio booths, working six innings on TV and three on radio. Even though he had become a TV icon, there was still nothing quite like radio for Harry, and he relished his time in the WGN radio booth.

His trademark calls— "Holy cow!" and "Cubs win! Cubs win!" at the end of every Cubs victory, especially in the division-winning seasons of 1984 and 1989—became as recognizable as the oversized eyeglasses he sported. Attendance records also reveal that the Cubs broke box-office records during Harry's tenure at the Wrigley Field microphone.

I've always believed that when Harry Caray was at a ballpark, he was

exactly where he wanted to be, doing exactly what he wanted to be doing—
especially if that ballpark was Wrigley Field.

Harry was 68 years old when he took over as the Cubs' primary TV
announcer. But it seemed like he'd been there forever. And for a new
generation of Cubs fans who grew up with Harry, he was there forever.

chapter 12

THE PRESIDENT IS ON LINE ONE

TRACK 12

HARRY TOOK AN IMPORTANT CALL ON THE AIR IN 1987, WHEN HE RETURNED TO BROADCASTING AFTER SUFFERING A STROKE.

I

N THIS COUNTRY, we've enjoyed a long tradition of U.S. presidents taking an active interest in baseball. And why not? It's our national pastime. President William Howard Taft threw out the first ceremonial pitch on Opening Day 1910 in Washington, D.C. President Franklin D. Roosevelt let it be known how important baseball was to the national psyche during the early stages of WW II, when he gave Commissioner Kenesaw Mountain Landis his blessing for the games to go on. And of course, most politicians are well aware of the benefits of being seen at the ballpark. Even so, the following incident is truly remarkable.

Harry Caray was five years into his reign at Wrigley Field, with no end in sight. Then in February 1987, the seemingly indestructible Harry Caray suffered a stroke. He was 73 years old, and although he was in generally good health, it was serious.

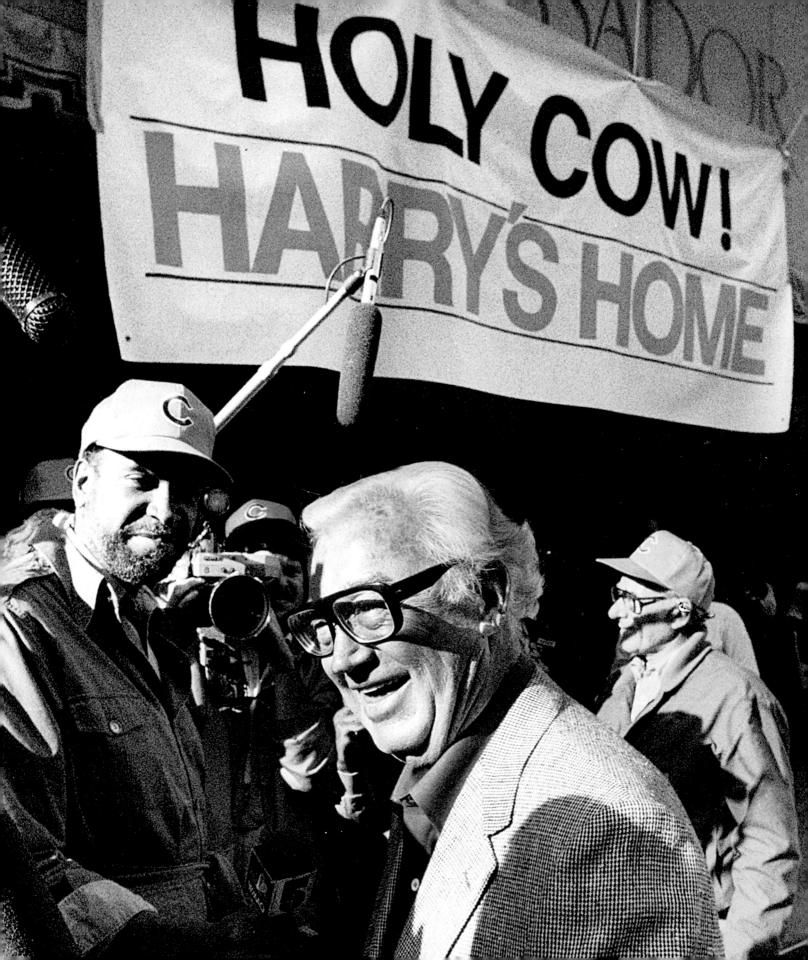

Legendary Chicago sports columnist Bob Verdi visited Harry at Harry's Palm Springs home and wrote a touching piece. Harry told Verdi that what gave him hope and what kept him going through the long days of recovery and rehabilitation were the cards and letters he received from loyal and concerned listeners.

Not just dozens of cards and letters. Boxes of them. Hundreds, maybe thousands, of them, all bearing well-wishes and messages of encouragement. Many fans told Harry how much he meant to them, and the hours upon hours of enjoyment he provided them broadcasting Cubs baseball.

Modern medicine works wonders, but when the human spirit gets buoyed by the kind of support Harry received from his fans, miracles can happen.

HARRY SHOWS OFF HIS NEWLY TRIM FIGURE, HAVING LOST **41** POUNDS AFTER HIS STROKE IN **1987.**

Harry missed the start of the 1987 Cubs season, marking the first time in his long run as a broadcaster that illness kept him out of the booth. In Harry's absence, the Cubs and WGN-TV employed a "Who's Who" of celebrity announcers to fill in, such as broadcasting legends Ernie Harwell, Brent Musburger, and Bob Costas. Comedian/actor Bill Murray added a zany touch perhaps never before seen in a broadcast booth as he shamelessly rooted for the Cubs and good-naturedly wished ill upon the opponents.

Finally, on May 19, 1987, Harry returned to the broadcast booth. It was Harry Caray Day in Chicago as this certifiable institution of the Windy City returned to his rightful place.

That wasn't all. While on the air, Harry received a very special phone call.

"Harry," the voice intoned.

"Hello?" answered Harry.

"This is Ronald Reagan."

Yes, it was the President of the United States, Ronald Reagan, an Illinois native and former sports announcer himself. In his radio days, he was known as "Dutch" Reagan. The Commander-in-Chief had interrupted his own busy day just to put a call in to Harry Caray.

We can't think of any other broadcasters who can say they fielded a call from the President of the United States during a ball game. That's how popular Harry was.

"Well, Mr. President, what a pleasant surprise," Harry answered, clearly touched.

"Well, listen, I'm just joining all your other fans across the country in welcoming you back on the air today," the President said.

"That's awfully, awfully nice," Harry said. "I really...Really, I don't know what to say. I certainly appreciate it, sir."

"I know it's Harry Caray day in the Chicago area, and it's great to have you back. You've had a lot of big-name celebrities fill in during your recovery, but there's no substitute for the real thing."

"Well, you're awfully nice. Thank you so much, sir."

Ronald Reagan became known as "The Great Communicator" during his presidency for his folksy manner and unique way of connecting with the American people. Come to think of it, that sounds a lot like a certain broadcaster we all know and love.

In late September of 1988, President Reagan visited Harry, in the WGN-TV booth, for yet another memorable broadcast. Their lives and careers paralleled one another. Both enjoyed mass appeal. It's fair to argue that the booth that day housed two of the great communicators of the twentieth century.

PRESIDENT RONALD REAGAN, A FORMER CUBS ANNOUNCER FOR IOWA RADIO STATIONS, THREW OUT THE FIRST PITCH AT WRIGLEY FIELD ON SEPTEMBER 30, 1998. HE THEN JOINED HARRY IN THE BOOTH TO ANNOUNCE THE FIRST PART OF THE GAME.

chapter 13

THE 1989 CUBS

THE SUMMER OF 1989 was doubly special for Harry Caray. First, his Cubbies won the National League East title for the second time in the decade. In the middle of that magical run, Harry made a July stop at Cooperstown, New York, to receive the Ford C. Frick Award.

TRACK 13

"DON'T YOU WISH YOU WERE HERE?" IN 1989 HARRY COVERED ANOTHER BIG YEAR FOR THE CUBS.

Just as they had in 1984, the Cubs of 1989 were coming off a disappointing previous season, and no one expected much.

But colorful and unconventional manager Don Zimmer had other plans. His "Boys of Zimmer" would battle for the division lead through most of the summer, before staking their claim in September.

The 1989 lineup featured many great and soon-to-be-great names including Ryne Sandberg, Andre Dawson, Mark Grace, and Greg Maddux. But the real thrill ride was provided by closer Mitch Williams, traded from Texas, whose nickname, "Wild Thing," was

(ABOVE) PITCHER MITCH WILLIAMS FLIES OFF THE MOUND ON THE WAY TO A SAVE AGAINST THE METS IN JULY, 1989.
(BELOW) RYNE SANDBERG UNSUCCESSFULLY THROWS FOR A DOUBLE-PLAY AGAINST THE METS IN JUNE, 1989.

everything it suggested.

Working the Cubs' season opener, Harry fretted along with Cubs fans everywhere in describing a ninth inning in which Williams walked the bases loaded, only to strike out the next two batters.

With the Cubs ahead 5–4, Harry captured the tension on the field.

"Two balls, two strikes, two outs, bases loaded, Cubs leading 5–4 ... Don't you wish you were here?" he told an audience that probably was holding its collective breath.

Finally and mercifully, the game ended: "He struck him out! Struck him out! Holy cow! Cubs win! Cubs win! Look at that picture of ecstasy on the field!"

That was vintage Harry, broadcasting as one of the fans, anxious, excited, and finally relieved, describing a tense, taut baseball game.

So it went all summer long, with Harry's calls mirroring the anxiety Cubs fans felt watching "Wild Thing" attempt to nail down the save.

The "Boys of Zimmer" played an exciting and sometimes odd brand of baseball that season. Imagine Harry's surprise when he'd describe one of Zimmer's hunch plays, such as a hit-and-run with the bases loaded. "Holy cow! Can you believe that?"

HARRY AND HIS WIFE, DUTCHIE, GREETING FRIENDS AT HARRY CARAY'S RESTAURANT IN CHICAGO.

The Cubs were on the road when they clinched the division title, in Montreal's cavernous Olympic Stadium for a night game with the Expos on September 26.

With the final out, Harry shouted: "The Cubs win the division! The

HARRY AND RYNE SANDBERG PARTICIPATE IN A MOCK PRESS CONFERENCE FOR 20 CHICAGO JOURNALISM STUDENTS.

Cubs win the division! The Cubs win the division!"

Alas, another Cubs postseason run ended in disappointment, as the San Francisco Giants, led by Will Clark, dispatched the Cubs in five games. Network television took over for the National League Championship Series, so Harry moved to the radio booth, where he was part of history again, as the Cubs played their first-ever postseason night games at Wrigley Field.

It would be Harry's last trip to the postseason as the Cubs' announcer.

chapter 14

COOPERSTOWN

H ARRY CARAY WAS a Hall of Fame broadcaster in the minds of his fans long before he received the Ford C. Frick Award in the summer of 1989.

But Harry wondered if he would ever get in. Hall of Fame voting, whether for players, managers, writers, or broadcasters, can be a political game. As popular as Harry was with his listeners, he no doubt had made a few enemies and ruffled a few feathers over the years.

Harry could be blunt and brutally honest on the air. He didn't care. Harry often said you can't fool the fans, so he never tried. If Harry was to be enshrined at Cooperstown, he wanted to go in on his own terms—meaning that he wanted to be able to enjoy the honor while he was still alive. He left explicit instructions with his son, Skip Caray (the voice of the Atlanta Braves) that if he were to win the Frick Award posthumously, Skip was to decline.

"He told me, 'If I wasn't good enough to get in while I was alive, I won't be good enough to get in when I'm dead,'" Skip recalled early in the 2007 baseball season.

Fortunately for Harry, his family, friends, and fans, the call finally came. Harry always said he wouldn't break down and cry during his induction speech, and he was true to his word. That doesn't mean, however, that Harry's acceptance speech was lacking in emotion.

Not surprisingly, the centerpiece of Harry's speech that day was the baseball fan, without whom, he acknowledged, there'd be no game.

"I look back on the 45 years of broadcasting the thrills of the wonderful game of baseball, which we all love so passionately," Harry said. "And then I think of the fan. And perhaps that's who I represent here today: you, the fan."

The crowd that day at Cooperstown broke out in applause. But Harry was far from done.

"We are all fans of the world's greatest game, baseball. And I know that it is the fans who are responsible for my being here," he said.

Even though Harry may have been contractually or financially beholden to radio or TV stations, or even the teams themselves, he knew his real boss was the fan who tuned in day after day, night after night.

"I've always tried in each and every broadcast to

serve the fans to the best of my ability," he said. "In my mind, they are the unsung heroes of our great game. The baseball players come and go. But the game goes on forever."

As big and as famous as he was, Harry knew that he, too, was a player on the bigger stage. But like all good players, Harry put on a vintage performance that Sunday in the bucolic setting that is Cooperstown. His voice boomed loud and strong and robust over the loudspeakers, the spectators nodding in knowing agreement with the sentiments he was so eloquently expressing.

"The players, the writers, the broadcasters, no matter how great, all are temporary actors on this stage," Harry said, his voice reaching a crescendo. "It's the game. It's baseball that moves ahead reaching new heights all the time, generation after generation. And I'm very, very proud of being some part of this important piece of Americana."

The day was a family affair for Harry. Accompanying him were his wife, Dutchie, his son, Skip, and his grandson, Chip, a then-up-and-coming broadcaster who would succeed Harry in the Cubs booth after Harry's death in February 1998.

"Speaking of pride, if you don't mind a little parental pride, there are

HARRY IS PRESENTED WITH A PORTRAIT AT WRIGLEY FIELD COMMEMORATING HIS ELECTION INTO THE BROADCASTING WING OF BASEBALL'S HALL OF FAME.

three generations of Carays here today," he informed the crowd. "My son, Skip, a great broadcaster in his own right in Atlanta and his son, my grandson, Chip Caray, who has just been named as the television voice of the Orlando Magic of the NBA. Yes, sir, baseball has given me many happy days and fine rewards. But this day, the day of receiving the Ford Frick Award, is the pinnacle, the zenith, the most important day of my baseball life. I feel honored and privileged today to be here with you. My wife, Dutchie, thanks you. My children all thank you. And from the very, very bottom of my heart, I thank you."

Harry was bursting with pride just a couple of years later, on May 13, 1991, when Harry, Skip, and Chip became the first father-son-grandson combination to broadcast a Major League Baseball game when the Cubs played the Atlanta Braves.

Skip has become an institution in Atlanta, and it's not inconceivable that someday, the three Carays can become the first and only father-son-grandson team enshrined in Cooperstown.

In receiving the Ford C. Frick Award, Harry joined a Valhalla of broadcasters that today includes his old broadcasting partner in St. Louis, Jack Buck, Mel Allen, and Vin Scully, as well as Chicago giants Bob Elson and Jack Brickhouse.

Each man brought his own style and color to the game of baseball. Yet none had more style and color than Harry Caray.

chapter 15

PERSONAL MEMORIES

AFTER SPENDING 12 years on Brewers' radio working with future Hall of Fame broadcaster Bob Uecker, I was hired in 1996 by WGN Radio to become the new radio play-by-play voice of the Chicago Cubs. By this point, Harry had shifted full-time to WGN-TV and only occasionally appeared on the radio.

TRACK 15

IN 1996 PAT HUGHES STARTED BROADCASTING FOR THE CUBS, WITH RON SANTO AND HARRY CARAY. HARRY'S VISITS TO THE BOOTH WERE A HIGHLIGHT OF PAT'S EARLY YEARS IN CHICAGO.

Whenever an announcer makes a move from one city to another, it is both exciting and frightening. You are thrilled with the opportunity, but everything will be different: a new group of people to work for, a new broadcast partner, a new radio station, and—scariest of all—a new audience for you to try to win over.

Moving from Milwaukee to Chicago was a gigantic career change. Milwaukee is one of the smallest markets; Chicago, one of the biggest. In 1996, Harry Caray was entering his fifty-second season of big-league

PAT HUGHES AND RON SANTO (STANDING) WERE FREQUENTLY JOINED BY HARRY IN THE BOOTH WHEN HARRY WASN'T ANNOUNCING ON TV.

announcing. He had worked in three different cities in his career: St. Louis (25 years), Oakland (one year) and Chicago (where, eventually, he would spend 27 years, 11 with the White Sox, 16 with the Cubs).

So he knew as well as anyone what I was experiencing in 1996. In spring training that year, I spent as much time as I could with Harry without being a pest. I was happy when we could just watch a spring training game without broadcasting.

When we were broadcasting, I made it a point to invite Harry to join Ron Santo and me on the air anytime he wished. Initially, Harry would decline. He wanted to give me all the space I needed. He knew I was trying to establish my own presence with the audience, and he didn't want to be seen as butting in and interfering. I reassured him he was always welcome on Cubs' radio and, over time, he stopped by very frequently.

In early May of 1996, on a cloudy Sunday at Wrigley Field, the Cubs played the Mets. In the fourth or fifth inning, Harry came over to the radio side for a chat. He loved doing TV play-by-play, but I honestly think he enjoyed radio play-by-play just as much, if not more. It was always a thrill for me to return from a commercial break and say these words: "With Cubs legend Ron Santo and Hall of Famer Harry Caray, it's Pat Hughes at Wrigley Field."

HARRY'S GRANDSON CHIP SUCCEEDED HARRY IN THE BROADCAST BOOTH IN THE 1998 SEASON.

Sometimes I would think, "Is this for real? Did I really say that? Am I really here? Am I actually sharing the Wrigley Field Cubs' radio booth with both Harry Caray and Ron Santo?"

I will always cherish the moment when Harry went out of his way to

say, on the air: "Pat, everyone loves the work you are doing. Sometimes it takes a while to find out whether they like you or not. This radio booth has been filled by some very fine announcers. I've heard you many times before. I know how good you are."

When he said that, my heart just filled with joy. After I thanked him, he said, "I don't say it unless I mean it." That was one of Harry's most endearing traits. He wouldn't say things unless he meant them. It was another reason the fans loved him so much. If he said something about a player or team, or a certain play or strategy, you knew you could take it to the bank. He was as honest as any broadcaster that ever lived. Long before Howard Cosell came along in the 1960s, Harry was telling it like it is.

That is one audio clip I'm very happy I saved.

Later that day, during the post-game show, I was either recapping the

scoring of the Cubs game or giving out-of-town scores when I was jolted by a bellowing voice: "How about those Cubbies?" Of course, it was Harry, but I wish you could have seen his face at that moment. He was 82 years old, but I didn't see an old man when I looked at him. Sure, he had gray hair and wrinkles, but he really looked more like a happy child who had just gotten his first bicycle. He was just so happy the Chicago Cubs had won the ball game. He never lost his childlike love of baseball.

In the two years we worked together, there were probably 15 to 18

HARRY AND FORMER CUBS ANNOUNCER JACK BRICKHOUSE EACH STAND ON THEIR "STAR" ON THE CUBS WALK OF FAME IN FRONT OF WRIGLEY FIELD.

games where Harry would sit in our booth and broadcast with Ron and me for the entire nine innings. These were the occasions when WGN-TV was preempted for a network telecast. Harry could have stayed home and taken the day off, which, considering his age, would have been perfectly understandable. But that wasn't Harry. If there was a ball game at Wrigley Field with a big Saturday afternoon crowd, that is where Harry wanted to be.

On July 12, 1997, Harry made a reference to his former Cardinals radio partner Jack Buck as Jack, Ron Santo, and I were waiting for the game to start. Jack was only a few feet away in the Redbirds' radio booth, separated from us by a large glass window. As Harry mentioned Jack, my mind raced back to the early and mid-1960s. My mom was from Columbia, Missouri, and my dad also had roots in the Show-Me State. On our summer vacations, we occasionally would head back to Columbia—Cardinals country to be sure. This was before the great proliferation of televised baseball, when Harry and Jack reigned supreme on KMOX and Cardinals radio.

That 1997 day at Wrigley, I mentioned that he and Jack were both in the Hall of Fame and that they formed one of the greatest broadcasting duos ever. Harry then shocked us with his own statement: "For my money, you and Ron are as good a radio broadcasting team as I've ever heard, and I don't say anything I don't mean."

I hesitated including the audio clip of Harry praising Ronny and me. I'm not sure why. Maybe I didn't want people to think I was showing off or tooting my own horn. But it showed how kind Harry Caray could be and how gracious he was to me. Several times during our two years

together he would publicly say wonderful things about me. I think he knew I thought the world of him, and I think he recognized how much I love baseball and its history.

If Harry Caray liked you, he couldn't do enough for you.

In 1998, the summer after Harry died, Sammy Sosa and Mark McGwire staged the greatest home run race in baseball history. If you're a Cubs fan, you might recall that the great Cubs broadcaster Jack Brickhouse also died in 1998, in August.

I knew both Harry and Jack absolutely would have loved to announce that Cubs season. What fun they would have had! After I made the call on WGN Radio of Sosa's 65th homer, I happily announced: "'Holy Cow!' and 'Hey-Hey' for Harry and Jack!"

Many major-league announcers in 1998 had a chance to make historic calls. I was there in St. Louis the night McGwire broke Roger Maris' single-season record with home run No. 62. I called all 66 homers Sammy Sosa hit that summer. And the Cubs made the playoffs in '98, just a

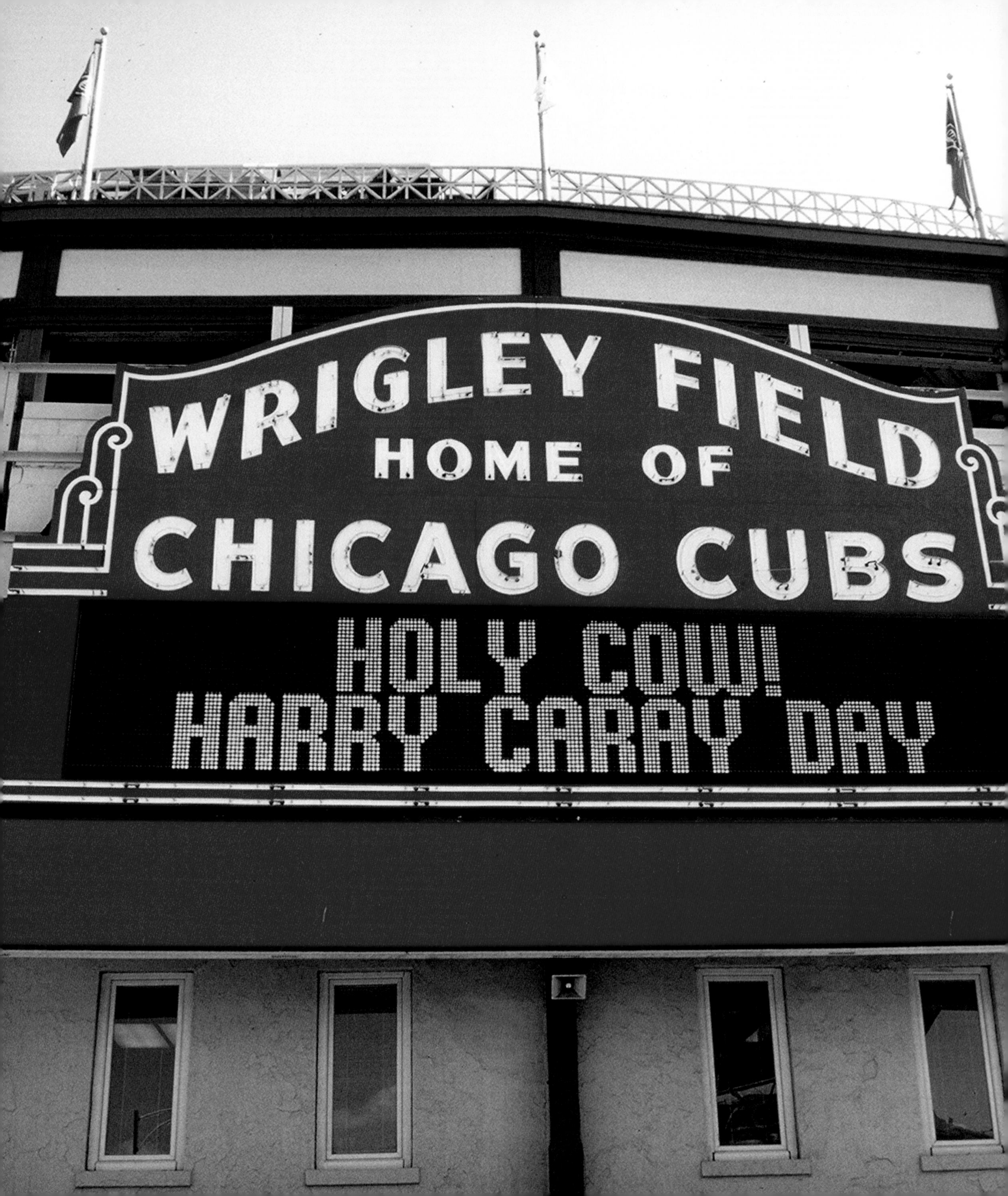
WRIGLEY FIELD
HOME OF
CHICAGO CUBS
HOLY COW!
HARRY CARAY DAY

year after beginning the 1997 season with an 0-14 record.

But when anybody asks me about my favorite call, or the one I'm most proud of, I immediately recall "'Holy Cow!' and 'Hey-Hey' for Harry and Jack" from September of 1998. I think Harry and Jack would have liked to have heard that one.

I miss talking to Harry. He was a wonderful storyteller. For instance, he would tell me about Jackie Robinson and his daredevil baserunning exploits. "Everyone in the ballpark knew he was going to steal a base, and he would steal it anyway," Harry said. "Watching him steal home was worth the price of admission. Pitchers used to brush him back with high, inside pitches, but he was almost impossible to intimidate. Besides, if he got angry, he played even better than normal, so they stopped throwing at him after awhile. It was brutal what Jackie had to endure those first few years, especially when the Brooklyn Dodgers were the visiting team."

Harry loved watching Willie Mays play baseball. This makes complete sense—Harry loved the game itself, even more than the teams he was working for. When Mays was hitting homers or working his defensive magic in center field, he was obviously thwarting Harry's Cardinals. But Harry was in awe of Willie.

"You should have seen him cover the outfield at the Polo Grounds," Harry would say. "The ball just jumped off his bat, especially when he was a young man in his twenties. His throwing arm was just about the strongest and most accurate of anyone I ever saw. He could do it all. In a rundown, he would escape about 25 to 30 percent of the time. I would cringe when he would come up in the late innings of a close game—unless he was facing Bob Gibson."

HARRY THROWS OUT THE FIRST PITCH AT THE 11TH ANNUAL CUBS CONVENTION ON JANUARY 19, 1996.

Harry saw Gibby's incredible 1968 season—13 shutouts and a legendary 1.12 ERA. "The best season I ever saw a pitcher have," Harry said. "Just about untouchable. People talk about his blazing fastball, but I think he got just as many strikeouts with his wicked sliders. One of the toughest men and talented athletes the Cardinals ever had. He would win a game a year with his bat.

"Sandy Koufax was, for a four- or five-year span, the most dominating pitcher I ever saw. Guys just couldn't touch that high fastball. His curveball would start at the top of your helmet and end up in the dirt. You knew early in the game if he had it going. If he did, the Cardinals were in for a long night. He needed only two runs to win most of the time."

Harry got to cover virtually the entire career of Stan Musial, "an amazing hitter. He would stay hot for three to four weeks at a time. He loved to hit at Ebbets Field in Brooklyn. I think he hit .500 there a few seasons. A great person and a great ballplayer."

When second-base great Ryne Sandberg retired at the end of the 1997 season, the Cubs held a day for him late in the season. I was the master of ceremonies, and Harry was one of the speakers for the pregame program. I remember him trying to convince Ryne to "stick around for one more year; you can still play this game." I think Harry loved to watch Ryne play because he was a throwback to a previous era in baseball. Sandberg was a modest team player, a gamer, and extremely talented. He was Harry's kind of player. In fact, Ryno was just about everyone's kind of player.

As much as I enjoyed listening to Harry Caray talk about ballplayers, I was absolutely enthralled when he talked about broadcasting. You can always learn from a guy like Harry. By the time I arrived in '96, Harry had over a half-century of broadcasting experience. He had covered championship teams, last-place losers, and everything in between. He was right on the money when he'd say: "You're lucky if your team is good. Not only will you have fun covering all the victories, but the audience will think you are doing a great job."

A great season brings out the best in an announcer. It is simply a wonderful experience and great fun to cover a good ballclub. But as Harry said, if the team is lousy, you have to try different things. "Don't make excuses for the players," he would say. "Have as much fun as you can to keep your audience listening. Treat each game like a special

event, and then forget about it. Come back the next day and do the same thing."

Every August I think of Harry's advice to give it your best during the season's dog days, for that's what separates the men from the boys. I completely agree. If your team is bad, August can be a very cruel month. You've already pumped out more than 100 games. You still have 50 or more to go. The weather in many cities is unpleasant. And team morale begins to sour on a bad club in August.

Harry was right when he said: "You've got to dig down deep and still give it your best performance."

One last memory is of Harry at the Cubs' Convention in January of '98. He stopped me and yelled out, "Hey, Pat," just like it came from one of my old high school basketball teammates. He had that rare ability to make you feel like you were one of his very favorite people. And I had only really gotten to know him in the last couple of years of his life. I wish I could have spent several more years with him.

When I asked him about doing anything differently if he had the chance, I found his comment intriguing. "I would spend less time being Harry Caray," he said. I think perhaps he regretted some of the things he did. I took his comment to mean he would have spent more time with his family and be more concerned with cultivating family relationships, but I'm not sure.

As time passes, I appreciate more and more the opportunity I had to work with this extraordinary man and get to know him as well as I did. He was one of the all-time greats. People like Harry come into your world once in a lifetime, if you're lucky.

chapter 16

FAREWELL

HARRY CARAY HAD a deep need for baseball, almost the way other people require food and sleep. He wanted to be at the ballpark even when he didn't have to be. He loved being around people and making them smile or laugh. He had no intention of ever retiring. Retiring to what?

TRACK 16

AFTER HARRY'S DEATH, "GUEST CONDUCTORS" CONTINUED HARRY'S 7TH-INNING TRADITION, STARTING WITH HARRY'S WIFE, DUTCHIE CARAY.

While out with his wife, Dutchie, dining and dancing on Valentine's Day 1998 in Palm Springs, Harry collapsed. He never regained consciousness. A few days later, the end came. When he died, it was a shock to us all, especially those of us who knew him personally. As his son Skip has remarked, Harry was larger than life; he seemed incapable of dying.

In the days after his death, Cubs fans paid their respects in ways Harry would have appreciated. Thousands of fans left flowers, candles, and Cubs memorabilia—even oversized black-rimmed glasses and beer bottles!—on the Harry Caray tile in the Cubs Walk of Fame. That would have made Harry smile, don't you think?

At the Cubs' spring-training camp in Mesa, Arizona, the Cubs held a nighttime gathering for the media, team officials, and players. The team's media-relations staff played a videotape of some of Harry's great moments as those in attendance smiled through their tears. Elsewhere, those who knew Harry got together and reminisced about the great man. All the while, the crowds around Wrigley Field and at Harry Caray's restaurant kept coming.

Harry's funeral was one of the largest in Chicago history. If it wasn't officially a "state funeral," it came close, as the governor of Illinois and mayor of Chicago attended, as did many baseball players, past and present. Undoubtedly, the number of people who turned out was influenced by Harry's gregarious nature. He had probably signed autographs for a good percentage of people who came to his funeral, an event marked more by celebration than by mourning.

Harry's dear friend, Pete Vonachen, delivered the eulogy. Not just any eulogy, mind you; one of the funniest, most touching and wonderful eulogies I have

HARRY SINGS OVER HIS BIRTHDAY CAKE IN MARCH 1997.

ever heard. Pete noted that among the qualifications for being a friend of Harry's were "unlimited stamina and a cast-iron stomach."

How often do you see a standing ovation at a funeral? That's what took place for Harry as the mourners stood and applauded. Afterward, those attending the funeral made their way to Harry's Chicago restaurant and toasted a few to the man they loved.

As I listen to his final words as a big-league broadcaster, at the end of the Cubs' dreadful 1997 season, I chuckle to myself. He says, "And the ballpark is still filled with people. What a wonderful way to end a season!" I did that entire season on radio, and the only wonderful thing about it

was the actual ending—the final out!

But his words almost make me feel that he knew that might be his final game, and he was just sort of pausing to reflect and just simply holding onto the moment before saying goodbye.

And how about his final line? It truly does exemplify the spirit of both Harry Caray and Cubs fans everywhere: "Harry Caray speaking from Wrigley Field. God willing, hope to see you next year. Next year maybe will be the next year we all have been waiting for forever."

INDEX

Aaron, Hank, 5
Allen, Dick, 6, 61
Allen, Mel, 5, 7, 97
Allen, Richie, 21
Allyn, John, 59
Ann-Margret, 73
Argint, Doxie, 26
Atlanta Braves, 93, 97
Barber, Red, 8
Baseball Hall of Fame, 41, 93
Battle Creek, Michigan, 31
Berry, Chuck, 73
Blue, Vida, 56
Boyer, Ken, 6, 20
"Boys of Zimmer," 87, 88
Brennaman, Thom, 50
Brickhouse, Jack, 97, 107
Brock, Lou, 6, 18, 20, 21
Broglio, Ernie, 18
Brooklyn Dodgers, 7, 109
Buck, Jack, 40, 41, 97, 105
Buffett, Jimmy, 73
Bunning, Jim 21
Busch Stadium (St. Louis), 6, 23, 45
Callison, Johnny, 21
Carabina, Chris, 25

Caray, Chip, 71, 95, 96
Caray, Dutchie, 71, 95, 97, 115
Caray, Harry
        Automobile accident, 45
        Birthdate of, 25
        Childhood of, 25–27
        Death of, 115
        Eulogy for, 116–117
        Father of, 25
        Funeral of, 115
        Move from Sox to Cubs, 75
        Road game re-creations, 35
Caray, Skip, 93–94, 95, 96, 115
Chicago Cubs, 36, 43, 48, 70, 97, 99
        Move from Sox to, 75
        National League East title
            (1989), 87
        1969 season, 15
        1982 move to, 70, 75–79
        1984 season, 11–15, 78
        1989 season, 78, 87–90
Chicago White Sox, 43, 69, 70
        1971 season, 48, 59, 60
        1972 season, 60
        1973 season, 62
        1976 season, 62, 64

1982 season, 65
South Side Hitmen, 64
Chicago (band), 73
Cincinnati Reds, 21
Clark, Will, 90
Cobb, Ty, 5
Comiskey Park (Chicago), 6, 59, 65, 69, 76
Cooperstown, 41, 93
Cosell, Howard, 102
Costas, Bob, 83
Cotton Bowl game (1960), 30
County Stadium (Milwaukee), 70
Cubs' Convention (1998), 113
Cubs Walk of Fame, 115
Davis, Jody, 12
Dawson, Andre, 87
Dernier, Bobby, 15
Detroit Tigers, 8, 71
DiMaggio, Joe, 5
Ditka, Mike, 73
Ebbets Field (Brooklyn), 110
Einhorn, Eddie, 65
Elson, Bob, 59, 97
Faust, Nancy, 69
Finley, Charlie 53, 56
Ford C. Frick Award, 87, 93, 97
Gamble, Oscar, 64
Garagiola, Joe, 40
Gibson, Bob, 6, 47, 109, 110
Gibson, Mel, 73
Gordon, Jeff, 73
Grace, Mark, 87
Green, Dallas, 76
Grudzielanek, Mark, 47
Hall of Fame, 41, 93
Harrah, Toby, 47
Harris, Arne, 48
Harry Caray Day, 84
Harry-Jimmy show
(with Jimmy Piersall), 64

Hartnett, Gabby, 12
Harvey, Paul, 30
Harwell, Ernie, 8, 71, 83
"Holy cow," 31, 33, 45, 61, 78
Hughes, Pat, 100–101
Isringhausen, Jason, 47
Jackson, Reggie, 56
Johnson, Walter, 5
Keith, Toby, 73
KMOX Radio-St. Louis, 5, 7, 21, 22, 27, 36, 105
Koufax, Sandy, 110
Landis, Kenesaw Mountain, 81
Larsen, Don, 12
Lewis, Jerry, 73
Los Angeles Dodgers, 8
Maddux, Greg, 87
Mantle, Mickey, 5
Maris, Roger, 107
Matthews, Gary "Sarge," 15
Mays, Willie, 5 , 109
McDonough, John, 71
McGwire, Mark, 107
McRae, Brian, 78
Melton, Bill, 62
Minnesota Twins, 60
Missouri Tigers, 30
Montreal Expos, 89
Morris, Johnny, 62
Murray, Bill, 73, 83
Musburger, Brent, 83
Musial, Stan "The Man,"
6, 37, 39, 110
Nen, Robb, 47
New York Mets, 23
New York Yankees, 7, 31
Norworth, Jack, 67
Notre Dame, 30
Oakland-Alameda County Coliseum
(Oakland), 56
Olympic Stadium (Montreal), 89

Orlando Magic, 96
Otto, Dave, 47
Owen, Dave, 14
Palmeiro, Rafael, 78
Pennant race
    1946 Cardinal, 35
    1964 Cardinal, 17–23
Philadelphia Phillies, 21, 23
Piersall, Jimmy, 64
Pittsburgh Pirates, 23
Polo Grounds (New York), 20, 109
Prince, Bob, 7
Reagan, Ronald, 84, 85
Reinsdorf, Jerry, 64
Ripken, Cal, 5
Riverfront Stadium (Cincinnati), 75
Rizzuto, Phil, 31
Robinson, Jackie, 109
Rogers, Kenny, 73
Roosevelt, Franklin D., 81
Ruth, Babe, 5, 6
Salas, Mark, 47
San Diego Padres, 14–15
San Francisco Giants, 56, 90
Sandberg, Ryne, 6, 12–14, 15,
    48, 87, 110
"Sandberg Game," 12–13
Sanderson, Scott, 48
Santo, Ron, 20, 50, 73, 100,
    101, 105, 106
Scully, Vin, 5, 8, 97
Selig, Bud, 70
Shannon, Mike, 19
Short, Chris, 21
Sosa, Sammy, 6, 48, 107
Sportsman's Park (St. Louis), 6
St. Louis Cardinals, 12, 19, 20, 21, 22,
    23, 27, 43, 109, 110
    1960s seasons, 41
    1964 team, 17–18
St. Louis Hawks, 29

Stone, Steve, 76
Street, Gabby, 35, 36, 40
Stroke (1987), 81
Sundberg, Jim, 48
Sutcliffe, Rick, 12
Sutter, Bruce, 12
Syracuse University, 30
Taft, William Howard, 81
"Take Me Out to the Ball
    Game," 7, 11, 19, 67–69, 73, 76
Tanner, Chuck, 60
Thomson, Bobby, 12
Twain, Shania, 73
Uecker, Bob, 19, 20, 99
University of Missouri, 29
University of Texas, 30
Veeck, Bill, 62, 64, 65, 69
Verdi, Bob, 83
Vonachen, Pete, 116
WCLS–Joliet, Illinois, 29
WGN Radio, 13, 73, 78, 99, 107
WGN-TV, 5, 7, 48, 83, 85,
    99, 105
White Sox Park (Chicago), 59
Williams, Mitch ("Wild Thing,"),
    87–88
Williams, Ted, 5
WKZO Radio–Kalamazoo,
    Michigan, 30, 31
WMAQ Radio, 62
Wockenfuss, John, 47
Woods, Jim, 23
Wrigley Field (Chicago), 6, 19, 70, 79,
81, 90, 100, 105, 116
WTAQ–LaGrange, 60
Zimmer, Don, 87
Zisk, Richie, 64